LEGAL CAREERS AND THE LEGAL SYSTEM

William R. Fry
Roy Hoopes

ENSLOW PUBLISHERS, INC.

Bloy St. & Ramsey Ave.   P.O. Box 38
Box 777   Aldershot
Hillside, N.J. 07205   Hants GU12 6BP
U.S.A.   U.K.

Library of Congress Cataloging in Publication Data

Fry, William R.
  Legal careers and the legal system.

  Bibliography: p.
  Includes index.
  Summary: Discusses the various types of lawyers, what
kind of work they do, in industry, private practice, and the
government, and how they work within the American legal
system.
  1. Law—Vocational guidance—United States—Juvenile
literature. [1. Law—Vocational guidance. 2. Vocational
guidance. 3. Occupations] I. Hoopes, Roy, 1922-
II. Title.
KF297.Z9F79 1988 340'.023'73 87-9298
ISBN 0-89490-142-7

Printed in the United States of America

10 9 8 7 6 5 4 3 2 1

Contents

1

Introduction

We are used to electing our mayors, governors, and school board directors. We are also used to complaining to them, or about them, when we please. We may not think it is special to go to the supermarket and find lettuce in winter (although we may be aware that it is grown 3,000 miles away and shipped in). We also know that if we rent an apartment and the landlord does not keep it warm, or fix a leaking roof, we can complain and force repairs to be made.

These everyday matters are not usually thought of as involving legal rights—we consider such things to be routine. We tend to forget that the legal system in our country has a major impact on the economy, on social values, on our rights, and on our daily lives. It reaches everything and everyone, and even when we have no problems with the law, it is at work, behind the scenes, to influence our values; the framework of our schools, businesses, professions, trades, and family life; and the right to speak our mind, not to be pushed around by the government, and to elect our leaders. As Barnard Swartz, a legal historian, said: "The true American contribution to human progress has not been in technology, economics or culture; it has been in developing the notion of law as a check on power. American society has been dominated by law as no other society in history has been. Struggles over power that in other countries have called forth regiments of troops in this country call forth battalions of lawyers."

It is the law which permits us to elect our leaders; and it is the law which protects our right to criticize them. Without laws, a farmer might not be able to ship his produce to us. And without the laws passed by our elected officials, landlords would not have to keep their buildings warm and safe.

Other countries have legal systems different from ours. Through history, people have seldom had a right to elect their leaders, and they certainly have had little right to complain about those leaders. Under the laws of many nations such complaining is a crime. Also, it is not a right of a farmer in every country to ship his lettuce anywhere he wants. If you knew how many laws were involved in this country for a head of lettuce to reach you—laws of interstate shipping, of trucking, of pesticides, and of prices—you might consider winter lettuce a miracle.

We have a legal system in which people elect their leaders and the leaders pass laws about how society is to function. People are permitted to argue about laws before they are passed, and to argue about what they mean after they are passed. We are an arguing society, and it is one of our sources of strength that almost no one can say to a citizen of the United States, "Keep quiet; you cannot dispute the rules."

This book is about the legal system and about lawyers, who have a most important role in that system. It is also about advocacy—a tradition in the law that gives people the right to argue for what they want. For reasons this book will explain, lawyers help in advocacy—they take people's sides in dealing with problems.

Samuel Riley Pierce, Jr., combined careers in government and private law practice that led to a Cabinet appointment as President Ronald Reagan's secretary of housing and urban development. Pierce graduated from Cornell University Law School and later earned an LL.M. from New York University Law School. Before his Cabinet appointment in 1981 he was general counsel of the U.S. Treasury, a judge in the New York Court of General Sessions, assistant U.S. district attorney for New York, and a senior partner in the New York law firm of Battle, Fowler, Jaffin, Pierce, and Kheel.

If you have ever wished someone would take your side, argue that you were right, explain why you did something, and protect you against harm, you know the importance of advocacy. The advocacy concept is fundamental to our system of justice—the way we settle disputes and protect individuals against unfairness by the government. In ancient times, disputes were settled by force, and even today there are countries where the government can do anything it chooses to its citizens. Our system is different. It says that everyone is entitled to be heard, that the government should not force people to do things without first letting them defend and argue and explain. In our system of justice, nothing can be done to or against a person without this chance, and no decision will be made to send someone to jail, impose a fine, or take away property until the accused person has been heard.

Lawyers do not decide about rights or punishments or who wins and loses a dispute. They help both sides in a dispute to have the best arguments on their behalf put forward. Lawyers are experts in how to argue, how to present explanations for what a person has done, or how to make the strongest case for letting a person do something.

Thus, our system of government is based on laws and on fairness, and lawyers contribute one key to the system: the right of every person to argue, explain, and be heard. This book shows how the legal system works, what lawyers do within that system, and how a person might choose a career in the legal profession.

2

The Roots of the American Legal System

There are more lawyers, judges, and laws in America than in any other country in the world. We use the law not only to govern ourselves politically but to solve social problems and regulate behavior in such areas as marriage and business. Our public officials, from the president to the town council, must make sure that their actions are lawful; even our leaders are required to obey the laws.

Common Law

The roots of the American legal system are in the English common law system, which is more an approach or a philosophy than a specific set of rules. Common law rests on the idea that there are permanent values which should govern the way citizens and governments behave. These values or principles constitute fixed truths which may or may not be written down. The flavor of this philosophy can be found in the Declaration of Independence, in which, in 1776, the leaders of the colonies stated why they were declaring their freedom from England. It begins, "We hold these truths to be self-evident"—a reflection of the idea that there are vital truths which people simply "know" to be true. It goes on to say "that all men are created equal," an example of the vague yet fundamental legal concept on which our government was founded.

For a country to rely on fundamental but sometimes unwritten and often vague concepts in the law, there must be a way to determine how the fundamental concepts apply to a particular situation. From England we inherited the idea that the courts decide this, and that judges, in settling disputes, apply a body of thought which has at its center these fundamental principles. The court decisions, as well as the principles they represent, are called the common law.

As a practical matter, there is always the possibility that different judges will disagree in their interpretation of an unwritten principle. In England, to avoid the chaos which would result from every judge's deciding what the unwritten rules were, there evolved the idea of precedent: that courts should be bound by the decisions of other courts so that there would be consistency in their decisions. People could then read court decisions and have some understanding of what the law is. Under this common law principle, judges are careful to review previous decisions of other courts in similar cases and to show how their new decision fits within the rule created by the old decision.

The Code System

The common law is the approach in England and in many countries which adopted the English system, including the United States. Many other countries, particularly in Europe, have a "code" system of law in which their legal administrators have tried to write down all laws in a simple and precise way. The theory is that all law will be found in the code, which does away with an unwritten (or "common") body of law that judges will interpret. In these countries, judges may apply the codes to a specific situation, but they are not considered to be creating laws.

In April 1982 President Reagan signed the bill creating a new U.S. court: the Court of Appeals for the Federal Circuit, the only national circuit court. All other circuit courts are confined to cases that originate in specific geographic areas. With President Reagan at the signing ceremony are (left to right) Representative Peter W. Rodino, Jr. (D-NJ); Representative Robert McClory (R-ID); Attorney General William French Smith; White House Counsel Fred F. Fielding; Howard T. Markey, chief judge, U.S. Court of Appeals for the Federal Circuit; Professor Daniel J. Meador; Daniel M. Friedman, chief judge, U.S. Court of Claims; Senator Robert Dole (R-KS); Senator Paul Laxalt (R-NV).

In a common law system, judges create the laws—often by claiming that the decision in the case is a logical or inherent result of a common law principle. There is an assumption in a common law system that codes (or statutes) do not necessarily cover all situations and that courts must fill in the gaps by applying common law. Common law judges may even declare statutes invalid because they violate common law principles.

As a result, judges and courts in the common law system have a great deal of power. And, as we will see, the American lawyer is expected to know or anticipate how the court is going to treat a legal problem.

Most "code" countries have constitutions, but our American Constitution was meant to be more permanent and fundamental than those of other countries; it is a reflection of our belief that there are permanent principles of justice that never change. And our legalistic approach to government led to a country which believed profoundly in the rule of law. Given this beginning, it was inevitable that, as the country grew, a complex, interrelating network of laws and rules would evolve. The United States is more "legalistic" than any other nation, and it seems certain that the complexity of American law will only increase.

Increasing Regulation

During our lifetimes, the amount of regulation by laws has increased at a staggering rate. There are whole new areas of society being brought under our laws: protection of the environment, rules about employing minorities, limitations on abortions, licensing rules for nursing homes, copyright provisions for computer software, controls on use of union trust funds, television and telecommunication requirements, and so on. As the world becomes smaller through technology and commerce, new rules are necessary to govern international trade relations. As high tech soars higher, there is a demand for rules governing how technology is used, how people are rewarded for their technological inventions, who owns the airwaves and the stratosphere, how we are to preserve our natural resources, and how the public interest is protected.

The country has also become increasingly aware of poverty and hunger and is sensitive to problems related to health, nutrition, and pollution. Reactions to these new concerns are translated into new laws, rules, and regulations. But the faith in the value and importance of laws inherited from our ancestors has not changed, and we continue to rely on basic laws to help us cope with a changing world. It is not surprising that the legal profession has had to find new ways to expand its ability to help people with their legal problems.

3

How the Legal System Works

Most Americans study the structure of the legal system in school and have some understanding of the courts, the legislatures, and the executive branch. They know that at every level of government there are three branches. The federal government has a Congress which legislates, three levels of courts (district courts, appeals courts, and the Supreme Court), and an executive branch headed by the president. Each state also has its courts, its legislature, and a governor, with state administrative agencies under the governor's executive branch. Each county has its executive branch, courts, and legislators, just as every city or town has a mayor and a body that makes rules.

Who Makes Our Laws

It is sometimes taught in schools that legislators make laws, that the executive enforces them, and that the courts settle disputes between people about the law. Unfortunately, it is

Federal Judicial System

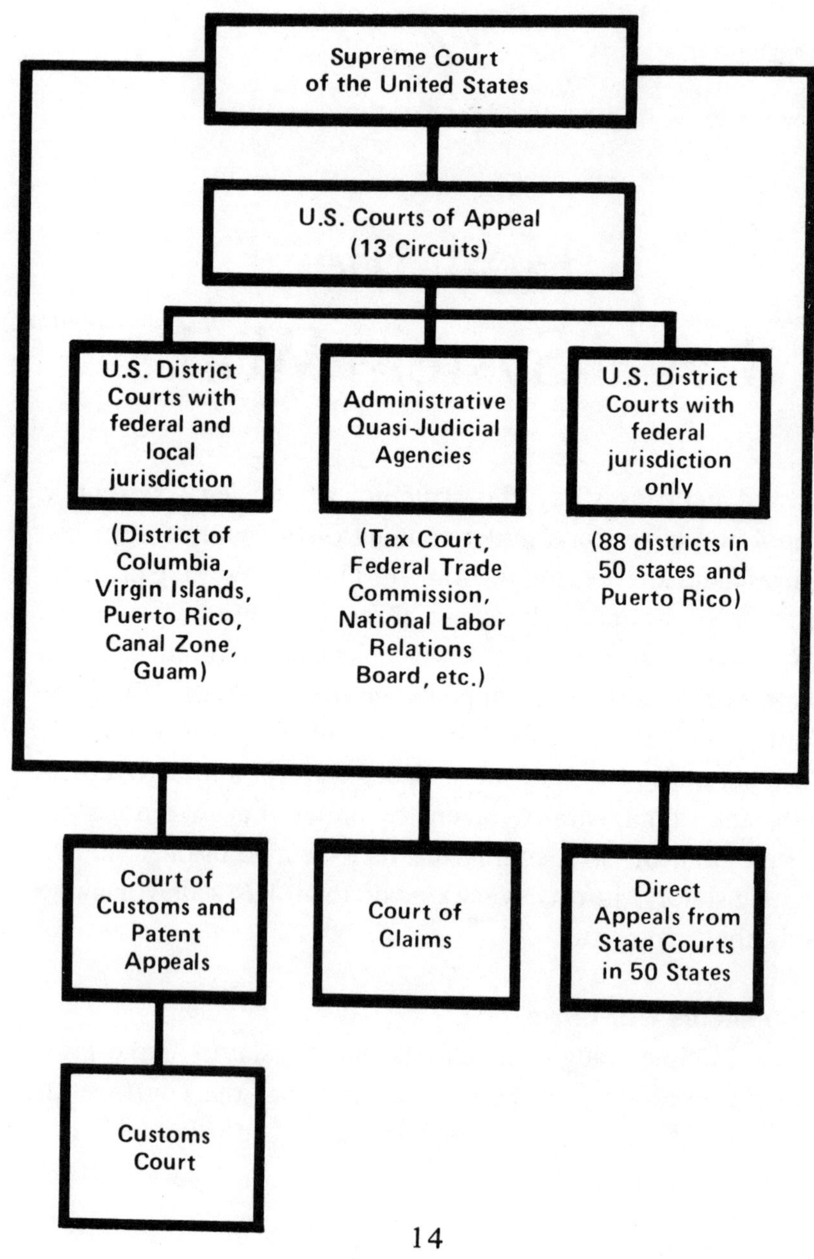

State Judicial System

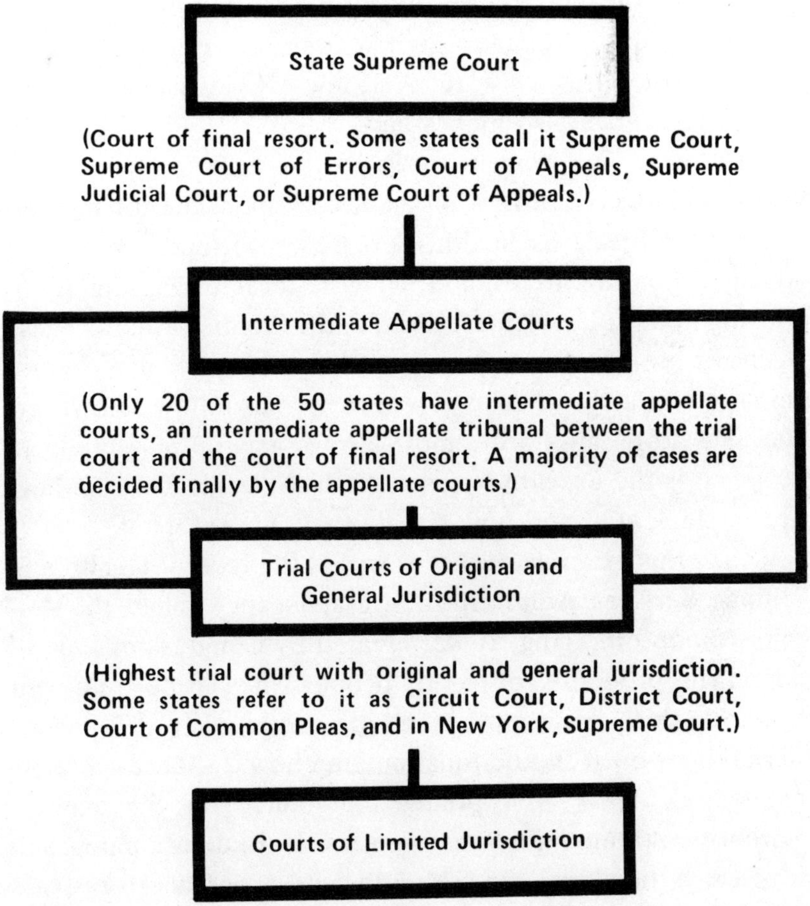

State Supreme Court

(Court of final resort. Some states call it Supreme Court, Supreme Court of Errors, Court of Appeals, Supreme Judicial Court, or Supreme Court of Appeals.)

Intermediate Appellate Courts

(Only 20 of the 50 states have intermediate appellate courts, an intermediate appellate tribunal between the trial court and the court of final resort. A majority of cases are decided finally by the appellate courts.)

Trial Courts of Original and
General Jurisdiction

(Highest trial court with original and general jurisdiction. Some states refer to it as Circuit Court, District Court, Court of Common Pleas, and in New York, Supreme Court.)

Courts of Limited Jurisdiction

not that simple. Legislators, of course, pass the endless numbers of statutes governing our activities in health, the environment, technology, and so forth. But judges also make law when they interpret a statute to cover a situation legislators never thought about—for example, when copyright laws covering authors' rights to their written materials are used to apply to computer software. And few people realize that the executive branch also makes laws.

The executive branch consists of the president (or governor or mayor) and a host of agencies responsible for regulating such subjects as health, defense, government property, aviation, housing, roads, and, on more local levels, sanitation, nursing homes, law enforcement, and consumer affairs. These agencies are usually created by legislators, who give them a mission and a set of rules to enforce or to follow. However, the legislators' laws are almost always general and broad in scope; it is the executive agencies which decide how the laws are implemented and how strictly they are enforced.

Take this example. There is within the federal Health and Human Services Administration a subagency called the Administration on Aging. It was created by Congress in 1964 to administer programs for elderly people. The statute creating it is about thirty pages long and describes what the agency should do, how it should function, and how it should spend its money. Congress appropriates the money for the agency. Within the statute telling the agency what to do is a paragraph which says that the agency should fund programs to provide legal service to the elderly. That is all it says. It is left to the agency to decide how to run the programs. An agency with such a vague assignment is forced to create regulations which fill in the details on what it does. These regulations must first be made public so people can comment on them; then they become law—just as much the law as a statute or court decision. In the case of the Administration on Aging, the subjects left to the agency to decide through its regulations include the following:

- who is eligible to receive the legal services
- what kind of organization will deliver the legal services
- what kind of staff the delivery system should use
- the kinds of legal problems to be treated or excluded
- the amount of money to be spent on this activity

Many Presidents of the United States have been lawyers. A recent lawyer to occupy the White House was Gerald Ford, who graduated from Yale Law School and practiced law in Grand Rapids, Michigan, before running for Congress.

As this example shows, much of the important decision making is left to the executive agency. And this is the pattern in our government: broad policies are set by legislators, and the details, often crucial ones, are left to the executive agency, which then makes additional laws which govern the details. From a lawyer's point of view, it is often the administering agency and its laws—not the legislative statute—that are the focus of attention in a legal dispute.

How Disputes Are Settled

Not only do administrative agencies share a lawmaking power with the legislatures; they share with the courts the power to decide disputes. Through a process called an administrative hearing, an agency of the executive branch may conduct what looks like a court trial. As the government has become more involved in the way society functions, the number of administrative hearings has increased. In 1976, after the Social Security Administration set new rules for recovering excess payments made to recipients of Social Security and related programs, 80,000 hearings were demanded by people who objected to being told to pay back money to the government.

On any given day in the federal agencies there may be administrative agency hearings dealing with a veteran claiming benefits or challenging a dishonorable discharge, a disabled person appealing a rejection of a claim for medical expenses, a radio station contesting loss of a license to operate, an urban renewal program complaining of a refusal to fund its housing projects, a stockbroker objecting to penalties for illegal sales of stock, an environmental group demanding to stop a company from dumping chemicals, and a trade group objecting to import tariffs. The federal government employs administrative law judges whose only job is to resolve these disputes, give a written opinion, and make a ruling, just as a court judge might do. And although it is possible to appeal the decision of an administrative judge, because of the expense and time involved for such an appeal the decisions of administrative judges are frequently final.

Our system of government is not as simple as textbooks sometimes make it appear. The executive branch makes laws and rules as well as enforces those passed by the legislative body; judges create laws in the process of settling disputes. Perhaps a better view of our three branches of govenment is that the legislators make the broad rules, the executive branch makes the more detailed rules, and the courts finally decide on the rules which apply between two persons (or a person and the government). The charts on pages 14 and 15 show the federal and state court systems. Federal courts can handle suits between people from different states, suits involving the U.S. Constitution or federal laws, and prosecutions for federal crimes. State courts handle most other cases.

Categories of Legal Problems

In some ways the law is a seamless web; a person with a problem who turns to the law for help may have no idea how to classify the problem, only a feeling that some injustice has occurred. Yet scholars of the law have tried to divide it into categories, partly because this makes it easier to discuss or to teach, and partly because different principles may be applied to different legal problems.

Private and Public Law. As we discuss later, there are some areas of the law in which lawmakers set rules to deal with disputes between two individuals—a kind of peacekeeping function. In other areas of law, the government has a more direct interest—it is more than peacekeeping between individuals; it is a matter of the general welfare of all citizens. In these kinds of cases the government may intervene; such cases are called public law because the public, through the government, becomes involved.

Thus, perhaps the broadest division in the law is between private and public law—laws for disputes between people, and laws where the government has an active interest. The lines are not clear, but one way to understand legal areas is to think of public and private categories.

Beyond that, there are other divisions. The following table gives limited examples of some divisions which lawyers might agree upon and which are often used in law schools to separate subjects of study.

PRIVATE LAW

Contracts	Property		Criminal Law	Constitutional Law
Sales contracts	Title to land		Arson	Civil rights
Credit	Leasing		Kidnapping	State rights
Employment	Mortgages		Robbery	Freedom of
agreements	Oil and gas		Murder	speech
Warranties	ownership		Perjury	Abortion rights

PUBLIC LAW

Tort Law	Family Law		International Law	Administrative L
Slander	Marriage		Hijacking	Environmental
Personal injury	Divorce		Outer space	laws
Trespassing	Name change		Arms control	Social welfare
Product liability	Support		War crimes	Taxation

These are but a few of the categories into which laws are placed. For the sake of explaining some subjects which often puzzle nonlawyers, let us look at torts and contracts.

Torts. Torts are acts which hurt other people physically or emotionally but which fall short of crimes. A tort is an action by one person (or company) which hurts another. The law says the person who is hurt may demand to recover for the hurts, usually in the form of money. Notice that torts involve two people (or companies, which are usually considered "people" in the law). The government is not a party to a tort case.

Contracts. Contract law also deals with private relations between people. But in contracts the basis of a claim by one person against another is that there was a specific agreement, either spoken or written, which has been broken. In contract cases the person complaining has to prove that there was a contract and that the opponent failed to do what was promised.

These categories in the law are not just academic; there are very different rules for contracts and torts, and still other rules for judging criminal conduct. But understanding how the law works should include an understanding that in real life problems do not come with neat labels on them. Suppose a person arrives at a lawyer's office and says: "I made a lease with Tom Taylor; after the first month he came around and called me a 'pig' and a 'cur,' wrote my mother a nasty letter, claimed I was making a mess, and pushed me against the sink. Then he sneaked a look at my mail."

Here we have a mixture of possible problems under torts, contracts, property, and administrative law. Which of these would be the ultimate basis of a claim would depend on the facts, the lawyer's analysis, and the readiness of the complaining person to bring a legal claim.

Perhaps these examples give a clue as to why the legal profession grew and why people considered it necessary to get professional advice about legal problems, which is the subject of the next chapter.

4

How the Legal Profession Grew

Part of the function of government of any country (or state or city) is to set rules on how people should behave, relate to each other, and do business together. There are some countries in which the rules set by government are relatively simple and easily understood. In West Germany, for example, there is a strict rule that all laws must be written into a code which anyone can read and that these laws must be clear and simple. Many contracts in Germany use standard forms developed by the government, so there is usually no need to employ a lawyer to write a contract. In some nonindustrial nations there are very few laws governing basic relations between individuals. People in these countries are expected to know, and to follow, custom and tradition. They are not expected to need written laws to govern how they behave. This is not, however, the approach taken in the United States.

In the United States, there are hundreds of thousands of laws. People's lives are affected by laws which cover how much tax they must pay, their responsibilities to people they live or work with, their rights to medical help or to certain treatment on the job, and the way they must conduct their businesses. People who own or work in a business also must follow rules which control how they hire and pay people, what benefits they must give, how they advertise what they sell, and the contracts they make to buy or sell products. And every year there are hundreds of new laws (or amendments to old ones) passed by the United States Congress and thousands of new or amended laws passed by the legislatures of all the states.

The First Lawyers

Centuries ago in England, people found that as the laws became numerous, they often could not understand or deal with their legal problems. This was particularly true for rich people, or nobles, who had money, employees, property, and land. These nobles began to use advocates, named from a Latin word meaning to "speak for" another person. The advocates would speak for, argue for, and interpret laws for their nobles. If a noble was summoned by the king into court, an advocate might speak for the noble in front of a judge and argue the noble's side of the case. Some nobles were said to be involved in so many disputes in different courts that they could not possibly appear personally at each one.

Since those times, laws have become even more complicated, and more people—not just the nobles—have needed help in understanding the laws. They also needed more than someone to speak for them; they needed advice on what the laws meant and how to obey them. Thus, in England, and later in America, more and more citizens came to rely on lawyers. In the United States in 1986 there were about 673,000 lawyers. They serve millions of people and businesses who need help in understanding the complexities of the law.

Specialization

Because there are so many kinds of lawyers doing different

things, it is difficult to describe what a lawyer does. Most lawyers specialize in one area of law because there is so much to be learned about that specialty that they must devote their whole career to understanding it. For example, a lawyer may specialize in domestic relations, which means all the laws dealing with family relations. These include laws on who can get married and what responsibilities married people have to each other; the duty of parents to support children; the duty of a husband to support a wife (or, perhaps, of a wife to support a husband); and laws about when and how people can get divorced and, if they do, who keeps the children, who pays for their needs, and who gets a tax deduction for the payments.

Another lawyer might specialize in real estate, which means laws about land and buildings. That lawyer will help people buy or sell a house or an apartment building, prepare the legal papers needed for buying or selling, or give advice to an apartment owner on what to do if tenants do not pay rent. The lawyer might also give advice on business accounting, tax liability, and insurance.

A law firm specializing in immigration will help immigrants to this country obtain permission to hold a job or apply for citizenship. If an immigrant is not in the country legally, an immigration lawyer may defend a suit brought to have the person sent back to the country from which he or she came.

Lawyers who specialize in business law may prepare contracts to purchase equipment, advise on how to obey employment laws, and help the company obtain loans from banks or issue stocks and bonds. The business lawyer will also help the company in its contracts with other companies and may give advice on such things as the laws limiting what a business can say in an advertisement. Because many businesses have to follow complicated government rules, a lawyer may also speak for the business when it has to deal with government agencies.

There are lawyers who specialize in running a city government or in contracts for defense work, or in laws governing hospitals or in the rules political candidates have to follow in raising money. Some lawyers work to prevent damage to the environment by industries which pollute waters or destroy forests; others handle civil rights cases dealing with race discrimination. There are even lawyers who specialize in advising other lawyers.

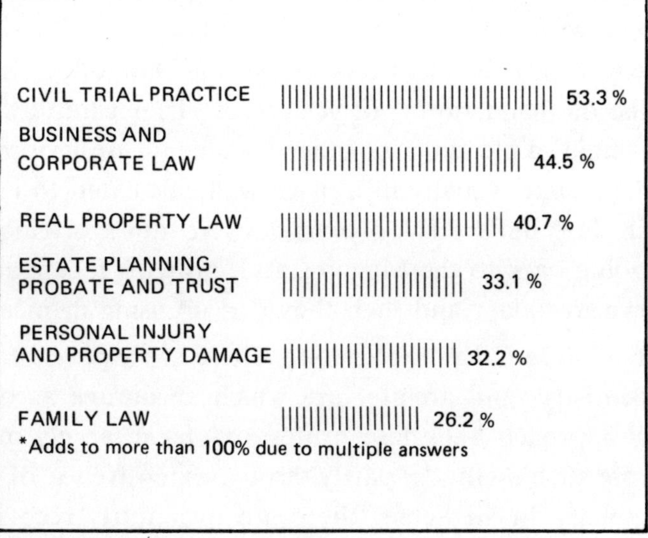

A 1986 survey conducted for the *ABA Journal* shows the most common areas of private civil law practice in the United States.

Law as a Cottage Industry

Lawyers work at many things. They are not, however, considered efficiency experts in the way they work. The practice of law has been called the last "cottage industry," meaning work still using the production methods prevalent before the Industrial Revolution. A cottage industry makes each item by hand, individually. Each is different; there is no assembly line and no uniformity. Craftspeople will design each rug or pot or leather jacket to be different from every other one. But by creating individual designs, they lose the efficiency of high-volume production. Lawyers today still believe in the value of individual design to fit the needs of a particular client for each piece of legal help. Like craftspeople, lawyers resist the use of machines to generate high-speed, uniform products, although lawyers are beginning to use computers to create their individualized services. In fact, until the recent arrival of paralegals (who might be called "legal nurses"), lawyers resisted sharing their work with anyone except another lawyer.

"Lawyers are handcrafters," says one lawyer. "They're much like the handcrafters of yesteryear. They carefully craft an agreement, a pleading, or other document, use it once and then put it away, usually in a place well calculated to inhibit retrieval. For hundreds of years they've done original research going back to the Magna Carta, bringing it . . . all the way down to today, and then they end up using it once."

Specialization in Other Professions. There are aspects of medicine, dentistry, and architecture which encourage a cottage industry approach.Yet these professions have largely moved away from such methods, partly through extensive use of para-professionals. In medicine, there are over thirty recognized occupations for which one must be certified after special training—for example, medical records librarian, nurse-practitioner, midwife, certified laboratory assistant, cytotechnologist, physical therapist, radiologist, and inhalation therapist. In dentistry, there is a similar array of helpers. A 1965 study revealed that there were 86,000 dentists who employed 116,300 full-time and 28,000 part-time auxiliary workers. In architecture, there is a recognized function for specialists in graphic arts, estimating, drafting, reproduction, administration, and specifications.

In addition to the use of paraprofessionals, there are areas of services where different professionals coexist. In the area of mental health, there are psychiatrists, psychologists, counselors, therapists, group therapists, and social workers. None is considered to be in the same profession as another, and one group has very little authority over another.

Paralegals. Until 1968, the legal profession resisted multiple levels of professionals and successfully limited the growth of side-by-side professions doing similar work. In 1968, lawyers accepted the idea of paralegals—trained nonlawyers who take over a share of the work lawyers previously did. Paralegals represent a step by the legal profession away from a cottage industry and may lead to the kind of diversification of tasks that other professions have accepted.

The use of technology (discussed in chapter 9) is another step away from the cottage industry. The practice of law is slowly evolving into a more efficient and responsive service for the public, although it will probably always retain something of its handcrafted approach to problem solving.

5

Anatomy of a Civil Case

The practice of law is often divided into civil and criminal law. The description below applies to civil law.

What do lawyers do when they have a case? One story recounts how a company having a serious disagreement with a federal agency spent months hiring one law firm after another trying to find a solution. Finally, the company approached a powerful lawyer who listened to them, picked up a telephone, and in thirty seconds obtained the result they wanted—for which he billed $10,000.

In other words, sometimes one phone call is enough. But, more often, representing a client on a case involves a series of steps, which include interviewing, investigation, research, analysis, negotiation, court hearings, and possibly a trial. Of course, not every case involves a dispute; sometimes a lawyer gives advice meant to avoid a dispute or merely helps a client comply with rules, such as the need to register a deed when one buys a house. The examples below are for a case where there is a real dispute with another person, or with the government. Here is a brief description of typical steps in such a case.

Interviewing the Client

A case almost always begins with a client presenting a problem to a lawyer or paralegal and asking what can be done about it. In the legal process, this is a vital and delicate time, requiring skill in interviewing. Clients do not usually know the law and cannot define the legal problem. They can only describe what is bothering them. Sometimes they are cautious about telling everything, and they may not know which facts are important. At the interview a lawyer must find out all the facts about the problem. It is also essential that a sense of trust be established, since the relationship between client and lawyer must involve full exchanges of information. A legal case can be lost at the interview through failure to bring out all the important facts.

Investigation Stage

Once a problem has been presented and a lawyer has agreed to take the case, the facts need to be checked. In a legal dispute, it is not enough for the client to say that something is so. The lawyer must locate evidence, or proof, that what the client says is the fact. The investigation stage may involve talking with other people, gathering documents, checking records, or taking photographs.

Legal Research

Once a lawyer has established what the facts in a case are, it is time to look at the law. This may involve finding and reading court decisions, statutes, regulations, and the legislative records about a statute to see what the legislators intended. It might also involve talking to legal experts, accountants, or social scientists.

Analysis

After a lawyer understands the facts and the law in a case, the two must be put together—a process that requires considerable skill. For example, suppose you stroll next door on a hot afternoon to swim in your neighbor's pool, skid over a roller skate lying about, and flip into the pool, breaking your leg on the way. The law says your neighbor is responsible for keeping the pool area safe for people who are invited. The facts are that you were frequently invited over, but this time you were not. Did your neighbor give you a standing invitation to come over any time? Did others have such an invitation, so you could argue that this was his practice? Did he know that you came over in the past when he was absent, and did he say that was all right? And even if you were invited, is leaving a roller skate near the pool so careless that it should be considered a menace to invited guests? These are facts which have to be merged with the legal rules in order for a lawyer to decide how best to handle the case.

Negotiation

In every case there is an opposing party; it may be an individual, a company, or the government. After an advocate has learned the facts and laws of a case, it may be time to negotiate. This means trying to persuade the opposing party to give the client all or most of what he wants. Negotiations may be a telephone call, a meeting, a letter, or any communication suggesting a way to end the dispute. Negotiation is primarily a process of convincing people to give up something, and it requires experience and skill. A negotiation should be carefully planned; offers and responses should be anticipated in advance.

Hearing Preparation

If negotiation fails, a lawyer will consider proceeding to a stage in which a third party (a judge in a court or a hearing officer at a hearing) will decide the dispute. Preparation for such an "adversarial proceeding" (in which both parties will present their positions) can be time-consuming. It involves deciding what arguments to make and in what order they should be made, presenting written or other forms of evidence, being prepared to cross-examine the opposing party or witnesses, and having a clear grasp of the facts and the law.

The increasing number of women in the legal system is illustrated by this session of the new U.S. Circuit Court of Appeals for the Federal Circuit. In 1980 there were only two female circuit court judges. Today there are eighteen. The three judges trying a case are (left to right) Pauline Newman, Helen W. Nies, and Jean Bissell.

Advocating at a Hearing

Court proceedings are more formal than administrative hearings, but both trials and hearings have the same goal: to convince the judge or hearing officer that the evidence and the law are on the side of the client. A lawyer should be prepared not only to present the client's case but to anticipate and argue against the evidence and arguments offered by the opposing party.

Appeals

Any hearing or court trial has the possibility of being appealed to a higher level. Administrative hearings can be appealed to a court; lower court decisions can be appealed to a higher court. An advocate's job is to assess the chance of winning an appeal, determine how much it will cost the client, and recommend whether an appeal should be taken.

* * * * *

Although most legal work involves only a part of this process, some cases go through all these steps. Lawyers who practice civil law will be ready to perform many or all of these steps for a client.

6

Criminal Law

Society prefers to let people resolve most problems between themselves. Civil cases are usually disputes between two people, or sometimes a person bringing a claim against the government. However, there is some conduct which society wants to prohibit, rather than relying on individuals to take action. In those cases, the government itself takes action as the party bringing the charge. The prohibited conduct is usually called a crime. Everyone is familiar with the dramatic crimes—burglary, robbery, arson, rape, and kidnapping, for example. There are lesser crimes, such as spitting in public places, serving tainted food in a restaurant, or chopping down trees in a national park. If the government did not act on the lesser crimes, probably no one would.

Federal and State Laws

Since we have two main levels of government in this country, federal and state, there are two sets of criminal laws. Most of the well-known crimes, such as burglary, murder, or robbery, violate state laws. However, the federal government also has criminal laws, which are usually different from those the states have. For example, matters affecting national security, such as treason and espionage, are federal crimes. Crimes involving the country's borders, such as smuggling drugs, or activities which usually cross state lines, such as kidnapping or hijacking, are also federal crimes.

The state and federal governments have agencies whose jobs are to pursue criminals, investigate criminal charges, and prosecute crimes in court. The federal agency which investigates crimes is the world-famous FBI, or Federal Bureau of Investigation. Most prosecuting agencies are called district attorneys, and virtually every city in the country has a D.A. responsible for representing the government in criminal cases.

Criminal Versus Civil Cases

The rules which apply to processing criminal cases in the courts are different from those for civil cases. Before mentioning them, let us identify the source of the difference. In a country which counts personal freedom as a great value, the loss of personal freedom, which can be the result of a jail sentence, is taken seriously. Although in a civil case a person can be forced to pay money, or lose property such as a car or house, this is considered less oppressive than being sent to prison. So the rules for criminal trials give defendants (those alleged to have committed crimes) many protections and rights. Some of these are:

- In a criminal trial the defendant must be proved guilty "beyond a reasonable doubt." In civil cases, it is usually enough for proof on one side to be "substantial"; a person can win in a civil case if it just seems more likely than not that he should win. A criminal defendant cannot be convicted unless it is all but certain he did the crime.
- In a civil trial, a person who wants a lawyer has to hire and pay for the lawyer. In serious criminal cases, if a

person has no money for a lawyer the state or federal government will provide one and will pay for it. This is to assure that no one is sent to prison without having every chance to defend himself.

- Defendants are protected by a number of special rules, aimed at stopping the government from treating defendants unfairly. Many of these rules are called exclusionary, in that they prevent the government from using evidence if it was obtained unfairly. For example, if a defendant is arrested and asked questions by police without being told that he can have a lawyer, the defendant's answers may be excluded from the trial—even if the defendant admitted doing the crime. Or, if police break into a defendant's house without a judge-approved warrant to search, anything they find which might be evidence of a crime may be excluded at the trial.

In television and fiction, criminal defense lawyers are romantic figures. In truth, the criminal law process is grim and seldom romantic. In most cities, the numbers of people

---

This 1864 painting by J. Morgan, a framed reproduction of which hangs in many lawyers' offices, is entitled, *The Jury.*

charged with crimes is so great that the courts are flooded. Most criminal charges do not go to trial, because the D.A.'s office and the defendant's attorney strike a bargain to settle the case, usually by the defendant's agreeing to plead guilty to a crime less serious than the one charged and getting a shorter sentence, or only a fine. In most criminal courts, well over half the defendants cannot afford a lawyer and are represented by lawyers working for the public defender, an agency which supplies attorneys, paid by the state, to defend poor people charged with crimes.

As Justice Black of the U.S. Supreme Court said, "There can be no equal justice where the kind of trial a man has depends on the amount of money he has." Our laws for criminal cases try to assure that, in a country which believes in the ideal of justice for all, no one is unjustly punished for a crime.

7

How to Become a Lawyer

Part of the increase in law school enrollments that started in the 1960s came from a sense that legal training has broad utility in business, government, and politics. While many who graduated from law schools become working lawyers, a good number do not, and many who start as lawyers shift to some other line of work.

John Folds majored in economics at George Washington University and lectured on economics there for 12 years, also receiving a law degree from the same school. But after going into law practice he decided he preferred the building business. In 1969 he founded Cumberland Custom Homes, which builds custom homes in the United States and Canada. Folds still has a law practice and takes an occasional case.

While it is still possible in a few states to become a lawyer through apprenticing to a lawyer and then passing the bar examination, this is declining, and almost everyone now completes college, attends three years of law school, and then takes a bar examination in order to be permitted to practice law in a state.

Law School Admission Requirements

Many graduate schools, such as those for medicine or physics, expect a student to have had a particular major in college—for example, mathematics, chemistry, or physics. For law schools, there is virtually no preference, and certainly no requirement except that a student should have done well at whatever was studied. Some people believe that, since lawyers work so much with words, the study of English is an advantage, and some consider knowledge of political science and government helpful. Law schools do not, however, set these as requirements.

I DON'T WORK FOR A LAW FIRM ‖‖‖‖‖‖‖‖‖‖‖‖‖‖ 39.8 % **ONE CANNOT BECOME A PARTNER** ‖‖‖‖‖‖‖‖‖ 16.4 % **1 OR 2 YEARS** ‖‖2.0 % **3 OR 4 YEARS** ‖‖‖‖8.1 % **5 OR 6 YEARS** ‖‖‖‖‖‖‖‖ 19.2 % **7 TO 9 YEARS** ‖‖‖‖‖‖ 12.4 % **10 YEARS OR MORE** ‖‖ 2.1 % Base — 615 Median — 3.9 years N/A — 0 Average — 5.9 years	A 1986 survey conducted for the *ABA Journal* shows how many years it took lawyers surveyed to become partners in their law firms.

In deciding whom to admit, law schools pay attention to test results on the Law School Admission Test, or LSAT, a national test that virtually all law schools require an applicant to take. The test attempts to measure comprehension and aptitude for legal reasoning. A good score on the LSAT, together with good grades from college, is needed for admission to highly competitive law schools. However, the law school boom in the 1960s caused new schools to appear and others to expand, so with the decline in applications in the 1980s, competition for places may be less fierce.

A popular movie and subsequent television series, *The Paper Chase,* dramatized law school as oppressive, purposely difficult, and painful. No doubt it is difficult for many, and it is often competitive enough to cause anxiety. The subject of law is, for most students, different from what they have experienced, and the way it is studied is also unlike the way most college courses are pursued. Law schools expect students to endlessly consider, decipher, and debate complex court decisions, and often there is no right answer to the question "What does this decision *mean?*" Work loads are heavy; law professors demand classroom recitation through asking tough questions, and the level of competing students is often high.

Nonetheless, it is possible to enjoy law school as a rigorous, challenging, and fascinating intellectual experience. And, of course, not everyone finds it difficult or oppressive. In truth, most graduate-level studies are hard work. Since law students are preparing for a career involving advocacy and contention with opposing lawyers, law teachers may introduce some contention into the classroom recitations, as drill. Except for that, law school is probably, among graduate schools, of no more than average difficulty.

Upon completion, a law graduate is still not a lawyer. There is a state bar examination to pass. The exam typically is two days long, involves multiple choice and essay questions, and is studied for by taking a special "bar review" course. It may seem strange for one just finishing three years of law school to need yet another course to pass the bar exam. Most law schools, however, tend to teach legal concepts and law from a national level, while bar exams test knowledge of local laws and practical workaday skills. Bar review courses teach these subjects, are usually about six weeks long, and are given by commercial bar exam trainers.

Law graduates can expect to have to compete for jobs, particularly those in big law firms which pay premium salaries. As of 1987, starting salaries in big prestigious law firms ranged from $45,000 to $65,000. Lawyers beginning elsewhere, in government or industry, may expect to earn $25,000 to $35,000 to start. Large firms in New York City and Los Angeles usually pay the highest. Similar firms in Washington, D.C., or Denver pay less but try to stay in range. Only about 5 percent of law graduates get these jobs. As mentioned, many who begin as lawyers will stray into other fields of work, and law is a profession more suited to such moves than, for example, medicine or research science. Law training teaches skills in seeing problems and solving them, in understanding complex rules about business or government, and in the discipline of clear written and oral expression, which are useful skills in many jobs.

A graduate from a top law school who has clerked for a federal judge usually has a promising future. After Joshua Rafner graduated from Stanford Law School (where he edited the *Law Review*) and served as a clerk for the Honorable Frank A. Kaufman, chief U.S. district judge for the District of Maryland, he was offered a job as an associate in the Washington office of one of the largest law firms in the country with 400 lawyers in Los Angeles, New York, Washington, and London.

The Nature of Legal Education

There was a time when law students learned their profession by working with a lawyer as an apprentice. In 1817, one of the first schools in the country for teaching lawyers was opened at Harvard University, in Boston. This school faced a peculiar problem. Apprentices had been taught law by working with a lawyer handling actual cases. A lawyer would talk to the apprentice about how the law worked and use the apprentice to help on whatever legal problems the lawyer had at the moment. But a school could not handle actual cases. Instead, the teachers had to try to explain what a lawyer did and what he had to know.

One decision made by early law schools was that the most important institution in our legal system is the court system. Whenever there is a dispute, it is a court which decides "what the law is." For example, if a farmer sells a horse to another person and the horse turns out to be lame, there could be a dispute when the buyer asks the farmer to give the money back. Whether the farmer has to return the money depends on the law. Is there a rule of law which says that a horse a farmer sells has to be in good condition? Or does the rule of law say that a buyer of a horse takes responsibility for checking the health of the horse? Such a dispute might end up in court, where a judge would decide what the law was and whether the farmer had to give the money back.

However, lawyers do not spend all of their time arguing cases in court before a judge. They spend much more time helping people understand legal rules and advising them what to do or not to do. For example, a lawyer advising the person about to buy the horse might say, "Be careful; if the horse is lame you will be stuck with it, so look the horse over carefully before you buy it." If the farmer sought legal advice the lawyer might say, "Don't say anything about what condition the horse is in; it is the buyer's job to look over the horse."

How does a lawyer know what to advise a client? A lawyer tries to find out what the law is by reading court decisions made in the past and assumes a judge will follow the rules found in those cases. Suppose the farmer's lawyer looks through the written decisions which judges have made and finds a case where a farmer sold a sheep that had a disease, and the court made the farmer give the buyer's money back. In that decision, the judge said, "As a rule, a buyer of livestock takes the risk for any defects which could reasonably be seen by any buyer. But in this case, the farmer said that the sheep was in perfect condition and when a seller says something like that, there must be a refund if the livestock is not perfect." The lawyer, when he reads this decision, perceives that the rule of law set by the judge is that a seller of livestock has to repay the money only if he *says* the livestock is in good condition. If he says nothing, then the buyer takes a chance.

Note that part of the lawyer's job is to decide that the sheep case is "the same" as the horse case. In other words, the lawyer decides that there is no reason to think that the rule is different for sheep than for horses or for a disease rather than a bad leg. On the other hand, the rule might be different for a bad leg than for a disease because one might be visible and the other not visible. A judge might decide that the buyer only takes the risk for what the buyer can see and the farmer has to pay back the money if there was an invisible defect. It is a lawyer's job to find out which of these interpretations is the law and to advise clients how to follow the law.

The law school at Harvard came to the conclusion that the most important skills a lawyer needs are knowing how to read the written decisions judges make and knowing how to understand the law as set forth in the court decisions. Because of this, the early law schools began teaching lawyers by what is known as the case method. This involved students reading the written decisions of judges and from this reading trying to understand not only what the rules of law are but why judges came to establish the rules they did. The cases which the students read were divided into subjects, such as real estate, tax law, divorce and family disputes, freedom of speech, and so on.

Of course, many laws are found in statutes—laws created either by the United States Congress or state legislative bodies. A lawyer can often find the rule of law by reading a statute. When a legal dispute goes to court, judges are supposed to decide the dispute by following the rules in a statute (if there is a statute which deals with the subject). Note, however, that it is still a judge who decides whether there is a statute on the subject and interprets what it means. And that is why, even though thousands of rules of law are found in statutes, it is considered essential that lawyers know what the judges have said in the past about these statutes. Law schools teach many things besides how to read and understand cases. They teach students to understand the meaning of the Bill of Rights in the Constitution, the powers and limits given to police officers in making an arrest, how to set up a business for someone, and how to write a deed for a house. Law school students are also taught how to write legal documents such as a contract to buy or sell something or an argument to be submitted to a judge about a case which is being heard in court.

Over the last ten years law schools have, in a very limited way, gone back to the idea of apprenticeship by arranging for teachers to take actual cases and permitting students to assist in the handling of the cases. These are called clinical courses, and they give students the chance to experience real legal work. Still, the original emphasis on the case method persists, and most of the training law students receive is based on reading and interpreting judges' written decisions.

A Typical Law School Curriculum

Law schools are less inclined today than in the past to require a rigid set of courses. Students are given flexibility to choose areas of interest beyond a few basic courses which they all must take. The following is an example of the kind of course pattern a student might pursue through three years of law school.

This is by no means a standard curriculum design; most students will, after taking certain basic courses, follow their own desires. Students have different inclinations and future plans, and they shape their studies accordingly. The next chapter considers what lawyers do and suggests the huge variety of jobs for lawyers.

First Year

Torts	Constitutional Law
Contracts	Administrative Law
Legal History	Ethics for Lawyers
Real Property	Trusts and Estates
Legislation	Legal Research

Second Year

Agency	Civil Rights
Corporations	Domestic Relations
Taxation	Litigation
Criminal Law	Evidence
Antitrust Law	Negotiation Skills

Third Year

Appellate Argument	Clinic in Consumer Law
International Law	Legal Philosophy
Environmental Law	The Laws of War
Clinic in Landlord-Tenant Law	Welfare Law
Rights of the Handicapped	Seminar on Taxation

8

Who Are Lawyers and What Do They Do?

Until about 150 years ago in America, people became lawyers simply by studying law with a lawyer until they knew enough to be able to claim to be a lawyer. There were no rules about who could be a lawyer. Abraham Lincoln, for example, before he became president, learned the profession studying with a local lawyer in his town, but he did not have to pass any test. Around 1835, however, some states began to make rules which prohibited anyone from practicing law who did not meet certain requirements. Illinois, where Lincoln was a lawyer, was one of the last states to establish "unauthorized practice of law" rules, which it did in 1910. Today all states insist that a person pass a test, called a bar examination, before working as a lawyer. The bar examination asks questions about the law. In some states less than half of those who take it pass, and people often have to take it several times before they qualify as a lawyer.

Legal Activities by Nonlawyers

Many people who are not lawyers must know a lot about law in their jobs. Policemen are required to make legal decisions before they arrest someone. The director of a city urban renewal project has to understand and comply with hundreds of laws about urban renewal projects, building codes, zoning, city planning, and contracts for construction. Others who are not lawyers draw up legal documents and give advice on legal problems. For example, if you buy a house, a real estate broker may prepare a contract in which you agree to buy the house at a certain price and under certain conditions. The broker will probably also advise about taxes, insurance, and mortgages. But strangely enough, there is usually a rule that the deed (which is used to legally transfer ownership to a house) must be prepared by a lawyer, although the deed is often an uncomplicated printed form and far less important than the contract. In the insurance business, very sophisticated contracts for insurance are offered to people by brokers, who will negotiate, explain, and make recommendations. Bankers also prepare important documents for people and give advice on banking rules and law.

How is it that all these activities which look like the practice of law are permitted? The answer is that lawyers, through their bar associations, have entered into agreements, sometimes called interoccupational treaties with a number of other groups, such as claims adjusters, bank trust officials, publishers, realtors, life insurance agents, accountants, collection agencies, social workers, and architects.

In that so many people use the law, give legal advice, and even have an understanding with lawyers that permits them to do it, how can "the practice of law" be defined? There have been many cases against laymen charged with unauthorized practice, but the opinions and verdicts rendered by the courts shed little light. In Florida, Rosemary Furman helped people who wanted a divorce obtain it for themselves. She gave them forms and information and showed them the steps they must go through. There is no rule against people obtaining a divorce without a lawyer. Moreover, courts have decided that it is acceptable to publish a book telling people about the law and giving them advice, or to give a course on the law to a group of people telling them how the law might apply to them. But in Florida Ms. Furman was told she could not help individuals obtain their own divorces. It was argued that she did more than supply people with a book—she gave them advice, and that amounts to "the practice of law." Thus, at least in Florida, it seems all right for a nonlawyer to help people handle their own legal problems but not to give advice during the process.

Some states permit nonlawyers to appear in lower courts, (such as justice of the peace or magistrates' courts) for other people. A few judges allow nonlawyers to appear primarily because the judge thinks they do a better job than a lawyer; for example, many paralegals are allowed to defend clients in landlord-tenant courts. And it is permissible for a paralegal to draft legal documents for an attorney. It is also permissible for legal documents (with blanks to be filled in) to be sold in drugstores; there is now a computer which asks questions on the screen about your wishes for your estate when you die and then produces a typed will for you to sign. In regard to "legal advice," which of these activities do you think involve such advice?

> If you spit on the sidewalk you might be arrested.
>
> You can get your own divorce if you complete this form I am handing you.
>
> I recommend you fill out this application and where it asks for additional remarks say: "none."
>
> I will represent you in small claims court in your suit against the landlord, if you pay me $100.

The first three statements would probably not be legal advice if given casually, but might be if given in an office by someone offering "legal help" for a fee. The fourth statement is not advice at all, but is an offer to give help. It comes close to an improper practice of law, but might be legal if said between two friends. Obviously, the question of what is or is not the authorized practice of law is not an easy one to determine.

In public sector law there is an area, often considered authorized practice, in which a layman can represent clients in administrative hearings. These hearings are not in courts but are held before an official of a government agency, who may be called an administrative judge or a hearing officer.

Administrative hearings are available to people dissatisfied with some ruling the agency has made, such as the denial of an airline route by the Federal Aviation Administration or a decision by the Health and Human Services agency to stop paying disability benefits to a person who claims to be disabled. The airline or disabled person can demand a hearing, in which they may argue, present evidence, cross-examine people, and ask the judge or hearing officer to decide in their favor. Most people do not know how to represent themselves effectively in such a hearing, and the rules for many government agencies allow a nonlawyer to assist the person. This permission to assist someone at a hearing goes beyond what happens at the hearing; the nonlawyer can, in fact, act as a "lawyer" to the person, long before the hearing, giving advice, helping prepare for the hearing, and writing legal documents and letters for the person.

It may be hard to define what functions are forbidden to nonlawyers, but it is easy to tell who is a lawyer. Every state licenses lawyers. Lawyers take their profession and their responsibilities seriously and have created many standards which they insist must be followed. Failure to comply can result in the loss of a license to practice law. The American Bar Association and the bar associations in all fifty states have passed rules of ethics to guide lawyers on such duties as vigorously advocating for a client, keeping communications with a client confidential, and taking responsibility for employees' actions.

Organizations of Lawyers

Lawyers' groups are called bar associations, and they exist on the national level, state levels, and in most cities and counties. On the national scene the American Bar Association (ABA) is the most prestigious, although national associations also exist for black lawyers, federal government lawyers, trial lawyers, and other specialty lawyers. The ABA has many committees which study areas of concern and often recommend positions on such matters as tax law or support certain

Many of our vice presidents have been lawyers. The most recent was Walter Mondale, shown here addressing a meeting of the American Bar Association. Mondale graduated from the University of Minnesota Law School and practiced law in Minneapolis before being appointed Minnesota attorney general, which launched his political career.

policies affecting the law (for example, the ABA has supported continuation of the legal services program for the poor, in opposition to President Reagan's desire to abolish it). While the ABA has no authority over state and local bars, its recommendations are compelling to those groups.

Bar associations provide a place for lawyers to consider matters of interest to the legal profession, to offer education to members, and to communicate policies to the public and to rule makers. In some states membership in the bar association is required of lawyers, but more often it is voluntary. Since lawyers hold many positions of influence and power, the voice of bar associations is listened to in legislatures and other places where actions may be taken which affect lawyers.

Bar associations also play an important role in the conduct of lawyers. They promulgate ethical standards, usually called Rules of Professional Responsibility. These are general principles about how lawyers, as professionals, should behave. The rules provide guidance and, when violated, can be the basis for a state to revoke a lawyer's license to practice. Complaints by clients about lawyers who misuse their funds, fail to represent them, or otherwise act unprofessionally can result in a hearing for the lawyers and subsequent suspension or cancellation of a license. It is a general rule that lawyers convicted of a serious crime of any sort cannot be allowed to practice law.

The Public Sector of Law Practice

Work in the public sector of law practice is in some ways merely another specialty, but it is sufficiently different to warrant description. Lawyers in such practice engage in some form of service, often pursuant to a government policy which directs that a designated group of persons be served by lawyers. The two biggest areas for this work are, on the civil law side, the offices of the Legal Services Corporation, and, on the criminal law side, the public defenders.

The Legal Services Corporation was created in 1974 by the U.S. Congress to take over the national legal services program started originally under the Office of Economic Opportunity (OEO). Using monies from the U.S. Treasury, the corporation funds about 300 neighborhood law offices around the country, which are nonprofit corporations that employ lawyers and paralegals to serve people too poor to afford a lawyer. Their clients are elderly or handicapped persons, minorities, children, and others in need. The problems they deal with are civil ones including housing, access to public benefits, education rights, consumer problems, divorce, support, and custody, and many others. The network of legal services agencies employs about 2,500 lawyers.

Similar to this program are other federally funded programs which provide funds for legal services to special groups, such as the disabled, Indians, migrant workers, handicapped schoolchildren, or immigrants. Under these various programs, there are usually a combination of nonlawyer advocates and lawyers, who provide assistance to people in applying for government benefits, in asserting rights against discrimination, or in other legal needs.

The public defender systems have already been mentioned. Both the federal government and the states finance the provision of lawyers for poor people charged with crimes. Two forms of services are used. One, called a staffed office, consists of an organization which employs attorneys (using government funds) whose job it is to represent criminal defendants who cannot afford a lawyer. The other form, often called Judicare (akin to Medicare for health services), pays private attorneys for providing this service. In large cities such as New York, hundreds of lawyers are employed to fulfill the

The Honorable Helen W. Nies, a member of the U.S. Court of Appeals for the Federal Circuit, graduated from the University of Michigan Law School. Before her appointment as a federal judge in 1980, she was a partner in the Washington law firm of Howrey and Simon, where she specialized in copyright law.

state's obligation to assure that every defendant in a serious criminal case has a lawyer.

Another public sector type of lawyering is found in what are called public interest law firms. These are groups of lawyers who come together for the purpose of dealing with problems of national concern, such as environmental protection, conservation of wilderness, health care, or veterans' rights. These groups sometimes represent individual clients but often do legal research and distribute policy positions or appear before legislative bodies to argue for or against a particular statute. They may bring "test cases," which are lawsuits designed to get a court rule on an issue of wide significance, such as the right of the government to deny disabled persons benefits without first offering an administrative hearing.

Public interest law plays an important role in our society, because often it represents the interests of unorganized citizens against the interest of powerful corporations with many lawyers on their side. For example, when oil companies want to lease land just off the nation's shores for oil drilling, many citizens are concerned about the effects of possible spillage. With the involvement of public interest lawyers, the legislators and courts which have to deal with such difficult issues benefit from hearing another side of the argument.

The Future

The practice of law changed little from colonial days to the mid-twentieth century. Lawyers were not permitted to advertise, and it was considered unethical for them to promote their services either by word or by deed. There were rules to govern what fees they should charge, how they should behave, and who could become a lawyer. However, beginning in the 1960s, new pressures were felt by the legal profession. First there was Legal Services for the poor, inspired by the Office of Economic Opportunity. Until then, the organized bar, while conceding it had an obligation to serve the poor, had not done so very effectively. Millions of poor people had no access to legal advice or representation. At the same time, a study done by the American Bar Association on the middle class revealed that there was a widespread need for services but that most middle-class people did not use lawyers, and many had a low opinion of them.

Another pressure on the legal profession was the post–World War II baby boom. During the 1960s, the law schools had to absorb thousands of young people who wanted to be lawyers and, with the help of postwar prosperity, had the money to pay for a legal education. The result was that, after too few lawyers in the 1950s, suddenly in the 1980s there were too many. Today America has more lawyers per person than any other country in the world.

Public Dissatisfaction with Lawyers

The Watergate scandal leading to President Nixon's downfall did damage to the American lawyer's image of respectability, since most of the culprits in that infamous episode were members of the bar. The public lost some of its faith in lawyers' regulating themselves and was ready to see a diminution of lawyers' monopoly over the practice of law.

Economic recessions in the early 1970s and again in 1980–1982 made the public acutely aware of how much things were beginning to cost, and lawyers' fees—sometimes $150 per hour—were felt to be excessive. This has led, for the first time, to open price competition among some lawyers, who advertise their services at fees far below what are normally charged.

Finally, new technology burst on the scene with a force which has yet to be measured or understood but has an almost frightening power to change how people and organizations function.

These factors have managed to change even so unchanging a profession as the law. Perhaps the most visible change has been the lifting of the rule against advertising. It started, as such things often do, in California, when a few lawyers decided to confront the problem that the middle class did not use or like lawyers. Their solution was easy access, low cost, and promotion. Several storefront law offices were opened in shopping areas; one came to be known as the "law boutique." These offices accepted charge cards, promised immediate help at low, fixed prices (one charged $9.95 for the first interview), and they advertised. The bar association tried to prevent the advertising, charging a violation of ethics. But in a suit originating in Arizona the United States Supreme Court ruled that lawyers could not be forbidden to make their services known to the public. Since then, lawyers have been increasingly and openly competitive, with commercials on television and in newspapers. Chains of law firms have opened nationally, backed by heavy advertising budgets. Law services are offered through Sears, Roebuck and other retail outlets, and there has been a general trend to merchandise law services in the same way as other services.

One of the first to take advantage of the Supreme Court decision (*Bates* vs. *State Bar of Arizona*) opening the way for lawyers to advertise was Joel Hyatt, who today presides over Hyatt Legal Services, a chain of more than 200 legal "clinics" with more than 600 attorneys who provide relatively inexpensive legal services to the public. The above photograph is taken from a Hyatt TV commercial.

Other changes have been less visible but no less dramatic. In 1977, a federal court in Virginia held that bar association rules instructing lawyers what fees to charge were in conflict with antitrust laws against monopoly and restraint of trade. Until that decision, the legal profession had felt free to "regulate" itself by setting fees all lawyers must charge—rules which, in any other business, would amount to illegal price fixing. But after the 1977 court decision, bar associations have been cautious about any conduct which might be challenged as tending to create a monopoly.

Less Expensive Alternatives to Lawyers

There has also been a movement by the courts and legislatures to permit nonlawyers to assist people. One 1982 decision of the California Supreme Court decreed that a paralegal representing a poor person in an administrative hearing had the same right (privilege) as a lawyer to refuse to reveal information a client had given him. Before this ruling (the first to grant paralegals a privilege), the only thing a paralegal could advise a client, as one judge observed, was, "Don't talk to me," because the paralegal could be compelled in court to reveal all that was said by his client.

Another trend is "alternative dispute resolution." It

Betty Franklin (left) and Von R. Hanton (right), paralegals in the District of Columbia Department of Human Services, confer with a client (center) about an administrative hearing.

comes partly from complaints that the courts are over-whelmed with disputes and partly from citizens who want less expensive ways to settle problems. Many disputes, from petty crimes to divorces to worker-employer disputes, can be solved in ways other than traditional court litigation. One alternative is through mediation, in which a person skilled at assisting people to settle their differences meets with both sides to help them reach an agreement. Another is arbitration, which is similar to an informal trial and results in findings and recom-mendations by an arbitrator. There have also been experi-ments with community courts, in which nonlawyer "judges" hear a dispute between people and make a recommendation.

All these devices try to avoid legal complexities and deci-sions based solely on what the law says. In an effort to avoid formalities and legalisms, alternative dispute resolution often uses nonlawyer judges, arbitrators, and advocates who under-stand some law but do not focus on traditional legal rules and are not hampered by legal technicalities.

The new concepts of group legal services and legal insur-ance were unheard of until the 1970s. Both ideas are well known in the health field, where hospitals and clinics arrange with groups to serve their members. Similar to health plans, group legal plans are contracts between a group (such as a teachers' group or a union) and a law firm, which contracts to provide legal services at a low fee. Union members may agree to a regular deduction from their wages to pay for legal ser-vices, just as is done for health insurance. The deducted amounts are paid to a law firm, which promises to assist mem-bers with legal problems, up to a certain number of hours.

The developments applying new pressures on the legal profession have tended to bring legal services closer to the public at prices it can afford. And the courts and legislatures are making it clear that lawyers will not be allowed to stand in the way of this progress. However, it may be that the development which will have the most impact on the legal profession is automation.

Computerization in Law Offices

The use of computers and communications technology is affecting all society, and the legal profession is not exempt. "Productivity of people in a law firm," says one New York lawyer, "can be greatly increased by the use of technology. A good secretary, typing on an electric typewriter, can type at a speed of sixty words per minute, or six characters per second. A memory typewriter has a speed of 150–450 words a minute; a jet printer, 950 words a minute; a laser printer, 18,000 words a minute. That is the speed of 300 secretaries typing a typewriter."

Here is the way the same lawyer, speaking at the New Roles in the Law conference in June 1981, describes the impact of computers on his firm, which has offices in New York, Washington, London, Hong Kong, and Tokyo:

> Melding our current technology into working teams has made it possible for people to be more productive and to reduce the number of people working on certain tasks. Indeed, we have a hundred fewer secretaries in our office than does another large New York law firm with the same number of lawyers. You can buy a lot of computers with the two million dollars a year saved by not hiring 100 secretaries.
>
> Our system is running twenty-four hours a day, five days a week, seventeen hours on Saturday and Sunday. We do all of this at a savings to clients, but we keep some of the savings for ourselves. Our printer's bills used to be higher than the legal fees in some cases. Now we do the printing in-house.

What does all this tell us about the law office's future? It seems clear that the one-to-one secretary/lawyer relationship is slowly being replaced by teams of lawyers, paralegals and secretaries working together.

One effect of technology in the legal profession can be seen in computer-based legal research. A law library contains thousands of books, some of them reference books which tell how to find other books, and some containing the many thousands of statutes, regulations, and court decisions. It often takes many hours of research in a library to find the law about a problem. Since not every office has a good law library, a researcher might have to travel to a library at a law school or a bar association.

Now there are several enormous computers in the country which have in their electronic memory hundreds of thousands of statutes, regulations, studies, guidelines, and court decisions. These computers can find categories of information in seconds. Lawyers can connect their own computers to these large computers by telephone. Once connected, they can command the computer to find laws and information on a particular subject.

In litigations involving millions of pages of documents, computers are proving invaluable for sorting through and researching the material. Once the documents are entered in a computer, it is possible to ask the computer to find a document which uses a certain word or combination of words, and in a few minutes the computer can do a search which would take a person hours or days.

Computers can also do creative analysis. For example, if one business is sued by another, one question might be the amount of money the first business lost because of some action of the second business. This can be solved on computers by modeling, which means the creation of a "picture" of the business on a computer, then asking the computer what might have happened "if. . . ." By changing basic figures in the financial model, the computer can be made to demonstrate what impact one business had on the other.

Providing legal services for a community the traditional way requires many resources: a library, file cabinets, secretaries, and copying equipment. With automation, an office can gain computer access to research banks, process documents quickly, and keep them in electronic memory files, thereby dispensing with many of the expensive resources required to support a traditional law office.

Since computers free people from reliance on a supporting clerical staff, it is possible to do at home work which once had to be done in an office. With computer linkages into an office and the capacity to do research and produce documents at home, there may come a day when lawyers will function away from a formal office setting, and a single lawyer can generate a volume of work once possible only in a law firm well endowed with library books, clerks, and secretarial help.

* * * * *

Despite the great increase in the number of lawyers over the past twenty years, society has absorbed them, and the opportunities show no signs of decreasing. Social problems, despite great efforts to resolve them, seem to continue and even to increase. The rapid changes in technology, and in ways of doing business in the face of automation and foreign competition, promise that the complexities lawyers must deal with will, if anything, continue to increase well into the twenty-first century. Just as the legal process has helped shape society in the past, the work of lawyers will have a major impact on the way we think and behave in the future.

Further Reading

Atkinson, Linda. *Your Legal Rights.* New York: Franklin Watts, 1982.

Bartholomew, Paul C. *Summaries of Leading Cases on the Constitution,* 12th ed. Totowa, NJ: Littlefield, Adams, and Co., 1983.

Cohen, Charles Z. *Your Future as a Lawyer,* revised ed. New York: Richards Rosen Press, 1983.

Dolan, Edward F. Jr. *Protect Your Legal Rights, A Handbook for Teenagers.* Englewood Cliffs, NJ: Julian Messner, 1983.

Friedman, Lawrence M. *A History of American Law,* 2nd ed. New York: Simon and Schuster Inc., 1986.

Fry, William R. and Roy Hoopes. *Paralegal Careers.* Hillside, NJ: Enslow Publishers, Inc., 1986.

Hyde, Margaret O. *Crime and Justice in Our Time.* New York: Franklin Watts, 1980.

Hyde, Margaret O. *The Rights of the Victim.* New York: Franklin Watts, 1980.

Lawson, Don. *Landmark Supreme Court Cases.* Hillside, NJ: Enslow Publishers, Inc., 1987.

Levine, Ervine L. and Elmer E. Cornwell. *An Introduction to American Government,* 5th ed. New York: Macmillan Publishing Co., 1983.

Lewis, Anthony. *Gideon's Trumpet,* revised ed. New York: Vintage Books a divison of Random House, 1980 (paper).

Lindop, Edmund. *Birth of the Constitution.* Hillside, NJ: Enslow Publishers, Inc., 1987.

Loeb, Robert H. Jr. *Crime and Capital Punishment,* revised ed. New York: Franklin Watts, 1978.

Meyer, Martin. *The Lawyers,* reprint. Westport, CT: Greenwood Press, 1980.

Munneke, Gary A. *Opportunities in Law Careers.* Lincolnwood, IL: VGM Career Horizons, 1986.

Weiss, Ann E. *The Supreme Court.* Hillside, NJ: Enslow Publishers, Inc., 1987.

Zerman, Melvyn Bernard. *Beyond a Reasonable Doubt.* New York: Thomas Y. Crowell Co., 1981.

Index